Everyday Writing

by
Bonnie L. Walker, Ph.D.

AGS®

American Guidance Service, Inc.
4201 Woodland Road
Circle Pines, MN 55014-1796
1-800-328-2560

Practical English Skills

Printed in the United States of America

ISBN 0–7854–0966–1 (Previously ISBN 0–88671–961–5)

Product Number 90881

A 0 9 8 7

Contents

Spelling Counts

Careful writers check their spelling. They correct any mistakes that they find.

 Read the paragraph. Check the spelling. Circle any misspelled words that you find. Write the correct spelling above each word that you circled. Use the words in the box. Then write the paragraph correctly on the lines.

Shoes

Their are shoes tooday for every ocassion. You can buy shoes especialy made for runing or joging. You can buy shoes especially made for walking. Every sport has its own special shoe. There are bowling, golfing, basketball, and basball shoes in any atheletic equipment store. Even with all the shoes around, sometimes the most poplar thing to do with shoes is to take them off!

athletic	jogging	running	especially	there
	popular	baseball	occasion	today

_____

_____

_____

_____

_____

_____

_____

_____

_____

_____

_____

For You to Do: Choose a story in today's newspaper to read. Look for spelling mistakes. Circle any that you find.

U
N
I
T

1

A sentence is a group of words that expresses a complete thought. You can put more than one thought into a sentence. You show where a written sentence begins and ends by the capitalization and punctuation of the sentence.

Three Sentence Facts
➤ A sentence begins with a word that is capitalized.
➤ A sentence ends with a punctuation mark, such as a period or question mark.
➤ A sentence does not end with a comma.

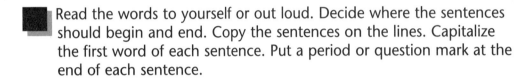 Read the words to yourself or out loud. Decide where the sentences should begin and end. Copy the sentences on the lines. Capitalize the first word of each sentence. Put a period or question mark at the end of each sentence.

You can be a healthy person you are in control of your life you can eat healthy foods when you are tired, you can rest or sleep every day you can take a walk or do some other exercise the choice of whether to smoke or not to smoke is yours perhaps most important of all, you can spend time with friends and family doctors say that happy people are healthy people

1. _____

2. _____

3. _____

4. _____

    _____

5. _____

    _____

6. _____

    _____

7. _____

    _____

8. _____

Alive! Sentences!

A writer has a choice of words. Choose words that say exactly what you mean. Choose sentences that make your ideas come alive!

To Think About

Which sentence do you like better? Think about your reason.

The dew fell softly covering the entire yard during the night.

Dew fell quietly last night over the whole yard.

A Find a more colorful word for each dull word. Write the letter of the matching word in the space.

Dull Words	More Colorful Words
1. _____ nice	**a.** laughable
2. _____ big	**b.** entertaining
3. _____ pretty	**c.** pleasant
4. _____ interesting	**d.** appealing
5. _____ funny	**e.** enormous

You can spice up dull sentences with more colorful words. Practice this skill in this exercise.

B Replace each underlined word or phrase with a more colorful or appropriate word. You may use the words in the box or think of words of your own. Use a dictionary to check their meaning if necessary.

tastier	starving	discover	preferred
arrived	satisfying	vociferously	

When I <u>got</u> home from work last night, I was <u>very hungry</u>. What a shock to <u>find</u> that we were having liver for dinner! I would have <u>picked</u> something <u>better,</u> like spaghetti. Nevertheless, with nothing else to eat, and my stomach growling <u>loudly,</u> I made myself eat the liver. Surprisingly, it didn't taste half bad. I guess when you're hungry, almost anything tastes <u>good</u>.

Dear Uncle Mac,
I would like you and Aunt Ola to visit us this year over the holidays.

I'd like that!

When something contracts, it shrinks. Words can contract. When we talk, we often use shortened words called *contractions*. Contractions use apostrophes in place of left-out letters. When we write, sometimes we use contractions and sometimes we write out the words.

A Write the letter or letters that have been left out.

Example: I am   I'm   __a__

1. you are	you're	_____		8. should not	shouldn't	_____
2. they are	they're	_____		9. would not	wouldn't	_____
3. we are	we're	_____		10. cannot	can't	_____
4. I would	I'd	_____		11. do not	don't	_____
5. I will	I'll	_____		12. does not	doesn't	_____
6. it is	it's	_____		13. did not	didn't	_____
7. she will	she'll	_____		14. could not	couldn't	_____

B Write out the words for each of these contractions.

Example: I'm   __I am__

1. he's	_____	8. they're	_____
2. we've	_____	9. they've	_____
3. can't	_____	10. shouldn't	_____
4. don't	_____	11. I'll	_____
5. you're	_____	12. it's	_____
6. I'd	_____	13. you've	_____
7. she's	_____	14. wouldn't	_____

Write It Out! Abbreviations

Abbreviations are another kind of shortened word. We use abbreviations in certain situations when we write. Most abbreviations have periods at the end.

Measurements

1 **in.**	1 inch
3 **ft.**	3 feet
2 **lb.**	2 pounds
13 **oz.**	13 ounces

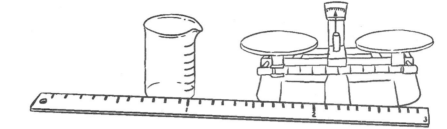

Titles

I saw **Dr.** Randolph yesterday.	Doctor
His name is Sam Barns, **Jr.**	Junior
Gov. Lewis signed the bill.	Governor

Names of Days and Months

Mon.	Monday	Jan.	January	Aug.	August
Tues.	Tuesday	Feb.	February	Sept.	September
Wed.	Wednesday	Mar.	March	Oct.	October
Thurs.	Thursday	Apr.	April	Nov.	November
Fri.	Friday	May	May	Dec.	December
Sat.	Saturday	June	June		
Sun.	Sunday	July	July		

 Rewrite the paragraph. Write out all abbreviations, except for titles before names.

Last Mon. Mr. Samuel Young visited his dr. The dr.'s name is Rachel Webster. Mr. Young hadn't seen Dr. Webster since the previous Oct. "I think you've gained 2 lb.," the doctor said. Mr. Young protested. "OK," the doctor said. "It's 1 lb. 15 oz." "That's better," Mr. Young said.

_____

_____

_____

_____

_____

_____

_____

_____

UNIT 1

Dates and Times

A.M.	ante meridiem	(before noon)	8 A.M.
P.M.	post meridiem	(after noon)	7:30 P.M.
A.D.	anno Domini	(Latin for "in the year of the Lord")	A.D. 1985
B.C.	before Christ		70 B.C.

Degrees from Colleges and Universities

B.A.	Bachelor of Arts	M.A.	Master of Arts
M.D.	Doctor of Medicine	Ph.D.	Doctor of Philosophy
B.S.	Bachelor of Science	D.V.M.	Doctor of Veterinary Medicine

A Answer each question.

1. Which came first? A.D. 1215 or 1700 B.C.? _____

2. What is the abbreviation for a veterinarian's degree? _____

3. Is Francis Smith, M.D., a doctor of medicine? _____

4. What is the abbreviation for three o'clock in the afternoon? _____

5. What is a B.A. degree? _____

Parts of Addresses

St.	Street	Ct.	Court	(before street names)		(after street names)	
Blvd.	Boulevard	Pk.	Park	S.	South	NE	Northeast
Pl.	Place	Apt.	Apartment	E.	East	NW	Northwest
Ave.	Avenue	La.	Lane	W.	West	SW	Southwest
				N.	North	SE	Southeast

B Rewrite the addresses. Write out each abbreviation.

1. 1214 N. Ellis Dr.   _____

2. 67 Park Ave., Apt. 3A   _____

3. 36 King Blvd., NE   _____

4. 3 Palmer Ct.   _____

5. 1607 E. 50th Pl.   _____

C Write the name of the state where you live. Then write its two-letter postal abbreviation.

My state is _____. Its abbreviation is _____.

Review Unit 1

Words to Know

Editing	the entire process of preparing the final copy of your writing
	Editing includes proofreading, revising, and recopying.
Proofread	to read carefully, looking for mistakes
Revise	to make changes
Recopy	to write again, usually to improve a paper's appearance

 Edit the paragraph. After making changes, recopy the revised paragraph. Look for run-on sentences and capitalization and spelling errors. Write out abbreviations and contractions. Look back to the other pages in this unit. Use a dictionary as needed.

Snowfall

How much snow is required for a major snowfall? What's a blizzard? It all depends on were you live, says Dr. gamble. In Atlanta, GA, one in. is enough. In Duluth, Minn., you'd need several ft. A blizzard is a snowstorm with high winds the wind blows the snows into huge piles called drifts. After a major blizard, you'll probley have to search for your car! people talk about a majer snowfall for years afterwards.

Snowfall

_____

_____

_____

_____

_____

_____

_____

_____

_____

_____

UNIT 2

Words to Know

Margin   the blank border around the edges of a page on the left and
                right sides and at the top and bottom

Indent   to move the first line of a paragraph in from the regular margin
                An indent is five spaces or about the width of your index finger.

A Open any book. Measure the margins of a page and write your
findings.

Top: _____   Left: _____

Bottom: _____   Right: _____

B Read the selection and divide it into paragraphs according to the topics.
Then copy the selection on your own paper. First, mark the margins on
your paper. Mark a 1" margin at the left side of the paper. Mark a 1"
margin at the right side of the paper. Mark a margin of at least 1" at the
top and bottom of the paper. Indent each paragraph.

Luis Chaves started his own business. He sells frozen pizzas. They are
called half-bakes. As you may have guessed, they are partly baked and then
frozen. Customers bring them home from the store and put them in their
freezers. When they are ready, people put the pizzas in the oven and bake
them about 20 minutes. When Luis needs a vacation, he likes to go skiing.
Every winter as soon as the first snow falls, he heads for the mountains. The
more it snows, the happier Luis is. After he skis, Luis enjoys sitting in front
of a roaring fire in the ski lodge. Luis says that his job and his hobby are a
lot alike. They start out frozen but end up warm and satisfying! Marcia Wu
has her own business, too. She owns a store that sells pet supplies.
Everything that a pet owner could possibly want for his or her dog, cat,
fish, guinea pig, hamster, or whatever can be found at Marcia's store! She
is very proud of the variety of products she has at her store. Marcia works
long hours because the store is open from 10 A.M. to 6 P.M. seven days a
week. She has two full-time employees and six part-time workers. There is
always unpacking, stocking, and cleaning to be done. When Marcia goes
on vacation, she picks a nice, warm beach. She likes to lie on the sand and
listen to the ocean waves. She says she wants her vacation to be the
opposite of her job—quiet and lazy!

Neatness Counts

Your handwriting tells something about you. Be sure to write so that other people can read your writing.

Form your letters carefully. Think of the space between writing lines as being divided in half.

A Write the capital letters of the alphabet carefully.

_____

_____

_____

_____

_____

_____

Write the lowercase letters of the alphabet carefully.

_____

_____

_____

_____

_____

_____

B There's an old saying: "Mind your *p*'s and *q*'s." A *p* looks very much like a *q*. How are they different?

_____

C Write the following using your best handwriting.

   Charleston, West Virginia

_____

_____

Be Letter Perfect!

Be sure to cross your *t*'s and dot your *i*'s. Write exactly on the line.

A Write each word using your best handwriting. Be sure your *m* doesn't look like an *n*.

1. Mom   _____
2. now   _____
3. where   _____
4. were   _____
5. Alice   _____

6. sweet   _____
7. country   _____
8. common   _____
9. Union   _____
10. music   _____

B Write each sentence using your best handwriting. Cross those *t*'s! Dot those *i*'s!

1. Jack drinks decaffeinated coffee.

_____

2. Caffeine is found in tea.

_____

3. We love the taste of an apple.

_____

4. Fruits are naturally sweet.

_____

5. Vegetables have lots of vitamins.

_____

6. Raisins are a good snack.

_____

Review Unit 2

> **Words to Know**
> **Proofread**   to read carefully, looking for mistakes
> **Revise**   to make changes
> **Recopy**   to write again, usually to improve a paper's appearance

 This paragraph has been written sloppily. There are spelling, capitalization, and punctuation mistakes. Some sentences do not end with a period. The writer did not indent the paragraph. Your task is to proofread, revise, and recopy the paragraph.

The First Day of Spring

In some places the weather is very cold and snowy in the winter. In those place, people realy enjoy the furst day of spring? On that special day, they wake up and look outside they want to see sunshine they want to see blue skies they go outside to get the daily newpaper and feel the warmth in the air. Its trully a glorious feeling.

_____

_____

_____

_____

_____

_____

_____

_____

_____

A Circle the word that is spelled correctly in each set of words. Use a dictionary if you wish.

Example: nessessary   (necessary)   nesessary   necesary

1. all right	alright	allright	alrite
2. sceince	science	scince	scence
3. beleve	beleive	belive	believe
4. furend	frend	friend	freind
5. begining	beginning	beginiing	beganning
6. accomodate	acomodate	accommodate	acommodate
7. sincearly	sincerely	sinceerly	sencerely
8. professer	proffesor	perfessor	professor

B The boldface words in the paragraph are spelled incorrectly. Cross out each boldface word. Write the correct spelling above the word.

                 athletic

Example: We enjoy ~~atheletic~~ events.

Our new **computor** is fun to use. The whole **familly** likes it. We keep information about the family's budget and schedule on the computer. My mother uses it to balance the checkbook and plan the **grocry** shopping. I particularly like it for **writting** letters. I write regularly to **sevral** relatives and friends. Cathy, my sister, **luves** the spelling checker. After she writes an essay, the computer searches for **mispelled** words. But the spelling checker can't help with some **misteaks**, like using *there* instead of *their* or *hour* instead *our*. My little brother Jamie's **favorate** computer program is a space game. He's always begging the rest of us to play with him. But he's so **gud** at the game that no one wants to play! Our computer was a good **investmint**.

Contractions

Recipe for Contractions
Step 1:   Take two words.
Step 2:   Put them together and remove one or more letters.
Step 3:   Replace the missing letter or letters with an apostrophe.
Step 4:   Presto! You've got a contraction!

Say these words out loud: **Do not**      **Don't**

A Write the contraction for each of the following words or phrases.

1. cannot _____
2. had not _____
3. did not _____
4. I will _____
5. I am _____
6. she is _____
7. we will _____
8. who is _____
9. could not _____
10. must not _____

11. does not _____
12. would not _____
13. should not _____
14. I would _____
15. it is _____
16. he is _____
17. we would _____
18. I have _____
19. you are _____
20. she will _____

B Write out the complete phrase for each of these contractions.

Example: it's _____it is_____

1. he'd _____
2. she's _____
3. who's _____
4. I'm _____
5. we're _____

6. isn't _____
7. you're _____
8. we'd _____
9. I've _____
10. doesn't _____

UNIT 3

Word to Know
Abbreviation   a shortened form of a word

When we write, we abbreviate words to save time or space. In formal writing situations, we write out the whole word. When we speak, we usually say the whole word.

Formal: "Hello, Reverend Brown."
Very informal: "Hi, Rev."

 Rewrite the following sentences. Write out all the abbreviated words. Use the words in the box.

Junior	ounces	February	Mister
page	pound	Thursday	Doctor

Example: Jack is 3 ft. 4 in. tall.

_____Jack is 3 feet 4 inches tall._____

1. Mr. Herman is a member of that law firm.

   _____

2. Jill Garvey was born on Feb. 21.

   _____

3. We would like you to come to a party next Thurs.

   _____

4. Mario Abruzzi, Jr., wants to be Dr. Abruzzi.

   _____

5. The kitten weighs 1 lb. 7 oz.

   _____

6. My bookmark is between p. 34 and p. 35.

   _____

Abbreviations in Addresses

Writing can be formal or informal.
>   A business letter is formal.
>   A quick note to a friend is informal.

Informal:	Formal:
Holly Powers	Miss Holly Powers
4105 W. Gerald St.	4105 West Gerald Street
Los Angeles, CA 90049	Los Angeles, California 90049

A Write your own name and address in formal style with no abbreviations. Place a comma between the name of the city and the name of the state.

Full name with title: _____

Street address: _____

City, State, ZIP Code: _____

B Rewrite each of the addresses. Spell out all abbreviations, except for titles.

1. Dr. Nancy Silvers
   121 Van Ralston St.
   Reading, MA 01867

   _____
   _____
   _____

2. Taylor & Wilson, Inc.
   12 W. 1st Street, SE
   Ocala, FL 34474

   _____
   _____
   _____

3. Mrs. Elle Eshbaugh
   8 W. Hagerstown Dr.
   Montgomery, Ala. 36110

   _____
   _____
   _____

4. Mr. George Osawa, Jr.
   359 S. Danville Rd., Apt. 2A
   Marshall, MN 56258

   _____
   _____
   _____

Special Abbreviations

R.S.V.P. —At the end of an invitation, people often write the letters R.S.V.P. They stand for the French phrase *Répondez s'il vous plaît,* or "Please respond." If an invitation has an R.S.V.P., you should let the person know whether or not you can accept the invitation.

C.P.A. —Diana Edwards is a C.P.A. That means she is a certified public accountant. She passed a state examination for accountants. The state certifies that Diana Edwards is a qualified accountant.
Correct: Diana Edwards, C.P.A.
Correct: Diana Edwards is a certified public accountant.

etc. —*Etc.* is an abbreviation for the Latin phrase *et cetera,* which means "and so on." We use this abbreviation to indicate that our discussion includes more items in a series, but we are not going to list them all.
Example: Grandfather Knott's farm had many animals, such as horses, pigs, sheep, etc.
Here, *etc.* means that Grandfather probably also had chickens, dogs, geese, cows, and other animals typically found on a farm.

Organizations —Some organizations are known by their initials. In formal situations, write out the complete name of the organization. In a paper, write out the complete name once. Then use the initials in all capital letters with no periods.

Some Well-Known Organizations
IBM   International Business Machines
NBC   National Broadcasting Company
FCC   Federal Communications Commission
NATO   North Atlantic Treaty Organization

Use each of the following abbreviations in a sentence.

1. R.S.V.P.   _____

2. etc.   _____

3. C.P.A.   _____

4. IBM   _____

5. FCC   _____

6. NBC   _____

Last Name First!

In everyday situations, we often need to write people's names.

My name is Tom Baskowski.   **Please spell that for me.**

Here are some common last names:

Smith	Levin	Diaz	Garcia	Stern	Owens
Rivera	Walker	Rogers	Hong	Jackson	Turner

A Use a telephone book for this activity. Look through the book. Find 20 common last names. Write them on the lines.

1. _____
2. _____
3. _____
4. _____
5. _____
6. _____
7. _____
8. _____
9. _____
10. _____

11. _____
12. _____
13. _____
14. _____
15. _____
16. _____
17. _____
18. _____
19. _____
20. _____

B Circle each last name in the paragraph that is spelled incorrectly. Write each name correctly above the misspelled name. Use a dictionary.

George Washinton was the first President of the United States. The second one was John Adems. Next came Thomas Jeferson. After him was James Madeson. The fifth President was James Monrow. The sixth was John Quincy Adamms. Can you name the seventh, eighth, and ninth Presidents? They were Andrew Jacksen, Martin Van Burin, and William H. Harison. John Tieler was the tenth President.

First Name Last!

First names, even common ones, can be spelled many ways.

  **I'm Kathy.** **I'm Kathie.**   **I'm Cathie.** **I'm Cathy.**

Here are some other examples:

Brian   Bryan   Lindsey   Lindsay
Stuart   Stewart Karen   Caryn

A Write the first names of 20 people you know.

1. _____   11. _____
2. _____   12. _____
3. _____   13. _____
4. _____   14. _____
5. _____   15. _____
6. _____   16. _____
7. _____   17. _____
8. _____   18. _____
9. _____   19. _____
10. _____   20. _____

B Write these first names. Use your best handwriting. Be sure to capitalize the first letter of each name.

1. Angela   _____   11. Masumi   _____
2. Brenda   _____   12. Niki   _____
3. Charlene _____   13. Patricia _____
4. Debra   _____   14. Perry   _____
5. Elizabeth _____   15. Raoul   _____
6. Fred   _____   16. Sean   _____
7. Gerald   _____   17. Sarita   _____
8. Hiroshi   _____   18. Thomas   _____
9. Julio   _____   19. Warren   _____
10. Laura   _____   20. Zeke   _____

Street Addresses

Writing your street address correctly is very important.

We write an address like this: 14 Jonesboro Avenue, Apt. 12.

Here are some names we give to roads:

Drive	Lane	Park	Parkway	Circle
Turn	Way	Street	Avenue	Boulevard
Road	Court	Highway	Route	Turnpike

Look up these words in a dictionary. Write their meanings on your own paper. Use each of the words in a sentence. Write the sentences on the lines.

1. Drive _____

_____

2. Turn   _____

_____

3. Highway _____

_____

4. Route   _____

_____

5. Way _____

_____

6. Park _____

_____

7. Street   _____

_____

8. Boulevard _____

_____

9. Turnpike _____

_____

10. Road   _____

_____

City, State, and ZIP Code

An important part of your address is the name of the city, the name of the state, and the ZIP Code.

A Follow the directions to complete this exercise.

Mr. George Legare
12314 W. Westcott Turn
Pompano Beach, FL 33062

Write the three abbreviations used in the address.
Then write out each full word.

Abbreviation   **Full Word**

1. _____   _____

2. _____   _____

3. _____   _____

4. Write Mr. Legare's ZIP Code.   _____

5. Write your ZIP Code.   _____

6. Write the name of your state.   _____

   Write its two-letter abbreviation. _____

7. Which one of these abbreviations is almost never written out? Circle your answer.

   a. FL   **b.** W.   **c.** Mr.

8. Which one of these abbreviations does not require a period? Circle your answer.

   a. DE.   **b.** W.   **c.** Mr.

B Write out the complete word for each of these abbreviations.

1. Hwy. _____   6. Dr. _____

2. Ave. _____   7. E. _____

3. NE _____   8. Ct. _____

4. SW _____   9. Pk. _____

5. St. _____   10. Blvd. _____

Review Unit 3

A Rewrite the paragraph. Write the complete phrase for each contraction.

I'd like to invite you to a party. It's a celebration of my birthday. You don't need to bring a present. I'll be treating you!

_____

_____

_____

_____

B Address this envelope to yourself. Do not use abbreviations.

C Write out the full names for these abbreviations. Use a dictionary if necessary.

1. FBI _____

2. AFL-CIO _____

_____

3. UNICEF _____

_____

4. UFO _____

5. UHF _____

6. P.O. Box _____

U N I T 4

To become a better speller, you need to practice these skills:

> ➤ Proofread your writing carefully.
> ➤ Learn to use apostrophes correctly.
> ➤ Identify vowels and consonants.
> ➤ Say words by syllables.
> ➤ Learn a few easy spelling rules.
> ➤ Recognize prefixes, suffixes, and root words.
> ➤ Check spelling in a dictionary.

A Find the mistakes in the paragraphs. Rewrite the sentences. Correct the mistakes.

At the dock on Friday, we saw several shipps passing by. They were on their way accross the sea. On ship was stoping at Le Havre, a port on the northwest coast of France.

I am planing to take a trip to France someday. I think I'll like being a world traveler. But I'd rather travel by plain. Ships are to slow!

_____

_____

_____

_____

_____

_____

_____

_____

B Write the letters of the alphabet that are called vowels.

_____

Write your first name. _____

Circle all the vowels in your name.

Part of proofreading is looking for words that are spelled incorrectly.

Here are a few proofreading tips to help you:

➤ Read the sentences out loud.
➤ Pronounce each syllable of "suspect" words.
➤ Check contractions and possessives.
➤ Check for careless mistakes.
➤ Don't rush. Take your time.

 Proofread the story. Find 14 spelling mistakes. Cross out each mistake.
Write the correct word above it. The first one is done for you.

   many
Like ~~meny~~ people, I love a parade! Years ago when I was a child, there

were lots of parades. I remember especailly the day that World War II

ended. It had been a long period of sacrafice for Americans. Many families

were seperated. Now the sacrifice was over. Famalies would soon reunite.

From inside my house, I heard music. Looking out the front window, I saw

a group of peple marching by. Evryone was waving flags.

  "Can I be in the parde, Mama?" I asked. I could see many of my friends

already in line.

  "Yes," she said.

  I quikly ran out and got a flag. We marched around the neighborhood,

cheerring all afternon.

  Later, I herd my mother calling me.

  "Vir-gin-ia!" She made it sound like three seperate words. I pretended I

hadn't heard her.

  "Virginia Ellen Rollins!"

  Even over the noise of the cheering croud, I could hear that! Reluctantly, I

left the parade and went home to denner.

Apostrophes

Apostrophes take the place of missing letters in contractions.
Apostrophes are used to show possession.
Apostrophes help form the plurals of letters, numbers, and abbreviations.

Possessives	**Ursula's** hat	the hat of Ursula
	the **clowns'** laughter	the laughter of the clowns
Contractions	I **won't** go!	I will not go!
	seven **o'clock**	seven of the clock
Plurals	I picked three **A's** and two **O's**.	

 Read each sentence. Identify each boldface word as a contraction, a possessive, or a plural.

Examples: Contraction   **I'll** be seeing you!
              Possessive   Did you see **Mom's** coat anywhere?
              Plural   I cannot count by **7's**.

_____   1. **David's** gloves are missing.

_____   2. Anita **doesn't** like tomatoes very much.

_____   3. When you leave, please **don't** forget your hat.

_____   4. Count your books by **2's**.

_____   5. "Mind your **p's** and **q's**," says Aunt Gretchen.

_____   6. On average, **men's** feet are larger than **women's**.

_____   7. Two of the most used letters in English are **e's** and **s's**.

_____   8. **Peggy's** friends are coming over to watch TV.

_____   9. **Who's** that waiting across the street?

_____   10. The **teachers'** meeting lasted a long time.

_____   11. I **can't** find Gina's recipe for chili.

_____   12. The **o's** are too small to read.

Vowels, Consonants, and Syllables

To be a good speller, you need to be able to recognize syllables.
A syllable is a word or part of a word with a single vowel sound.

Say these two words. Notice the difference.   catch   frozen

Circle the word that has more than one syllable.

The alphabet has two kinds of letters: vowels and consonants.
The vowels are *a, e, i, o, u,* and sometimes *y.*
All the other letters are consonants.
A vowel sound is represented by one or more vowels.

c**a**tch   The word has only one vowel sound, so it has only one syllable.
fr**o**z**e**n   The word has two vowel sounds, so it has two syllables.

A word may have many syllables, but each syllable must have a vowel sound.

p**o**w**e**rf**u**l   **pow • er • ful**
                              | | |
                              vowel sounds

Rewrite each word. Divide each word into syllables.

Examples: community   **com • mu • ni • ty**
                       grammar   **gram • mar**

1. swimming _____   11. regular _____

2. Skippy _____   12. Carmen _____

3. manual _____   13. paper _____

4. muggy _____   14. necklace _____

5. comma _____   15. power _____

6. magazine _____   16. purple _____

7. runner _____   17. sharper _____

8. pencil _____   18. mountain _____

9. computer _____   19. television _____

10. alphabet _____   20. reflect _____

Double the Final Consonant ... or Not

Some spelling rules require you to identify vowels and consonants.

Sometimes we double the final consonant of a word before we add an ending. Sometimes the final consonant is not doubled. In this lesson, you will learn two rules that will help you remember whether to double or not.

Look at these words: jog   set   log   bat   stop   slip

They have three things in common:
1. They are one-syllable words.
2. They end with a single consonant.
3. They have only one vowel before the final consonant.

Rule 1: When a one-syllable word ends in a single consonant and has only one vowel before that consonant, double the consonant before adding an ending that begins with a vowel.

Rewrite each word. Add the ending to the word. Double the final consonant only if the word follows Rule 1.

Examples: ship + ed   shipped   (double the final consonant)
                          sweet + ly   sweetly   (do not double the final consonant)

1. bat + er   _____
2. toast + er   _____
3. play + ing   _____
4. step + ed   _____
5. fit + ed   _____
6. plan + ing   _____
7. wrap + ed   _____
8. hem + ed   _____
9. hurt + ing   _____
10. beg + ed   _____

11. jump + ing   _____
12. top + ing   _____
13. slip + er   _____
14. clear + ing   _____
15. swim + er   _____
16. cut + ing   _____
17. plant + ed   _____
18. tap + ed   _____
19. drag + ing   _____
20. run + ing   _____

Rule 2: When adding an ending that begins with a vowel to a two-syllable word that ends with a single consonant preceded by a single vowel,

—double the final consonant if the second syllable of the word is accented.

—do not double the final consonant if the first syllable of the word is accented.

Two-Syllable Words, First Syllable Accented			Two-Syllable Words, Second Syllable Accented		
signal	+ ed	signaled	begin	+ er	beginner
pilot	+ ing	piloting	forgot	+ en	forgotten
number	+ ed	numbered	control	+ ing	controlling

A Rewrite each word. Add the ending to the word. Double the final consonant only if the word follows Rule 2.

1. permit + ing _____

2. admit + ed _____

3. flavor + ful _____

4. pilot + ed _____

5. commit + ing _____

6. equip + ed _____

7. forget + ful _____

8. differ + ence _____

9. begin + ing _____

10. order + ing _____

B Rewrite each word. Add the ending to the word. Double the final consonant if necessary.

1. shop + ing _____

2. offer + ed _____

3. nut + y _____

4. bat + ing _____

5. wonder + ful _____

6. wait + ing _____

7. plan + ed _____

8. design + er _____

9. regret + ing _____

10. teach + er _____

11. sit + ing _____

12. open + ing _____

13. laugh + ing _____

14. clear + ly _____

15. infer + ed _____

16. sun + y _____

Words with a Final *e*

When a word ends with a silent *e*, you must make a decision before adding an ending. Do you keep the *e*, or do you drop it? Here are two rules that will help you:

Rule 1: When a word ends with a silent *e*, keep the *e* before adding an ending that begins with a consonant.

Examples: safe + ty = safety   use + ful = useful

Rule 2: When a word ends with a silent *e*, drop the *e* before adding an ending that begins with a vowel.

Examples: large + er = larger   give + ing = giving

A Practice using Rules 1 and 2. Write each word with its ending.

1. love + ly _____
2. write + er _____
3. care + ful _____
4. hope + ed _____
5. lone + ly _____

6. write + ing _____
7. love + able _____
8. care + ing _____
9. hope + less _____
10. dive + ing _____

B Practice using Rules 1 and 2. Write each word with its ending.

1. practice + ing _____
2. live + ly _____
3. compare + able _____
4. use + less _____
5. surprise + ing _____
6. remove + ed _____
7. age + less _____
8. prove + ing _____
9. amuse + ment _____
10. chase + ing _____

11. skate + er _____
12. excite + ment _____
13. believe + er _____
14. waste + ed _____
15. arrange + ment _____
16. pale + ness _____
17. change + ed _____
18. advertise + ment _____
19. voice + ed _____
20. grace + ful _____

The *i* before *e* Rule

Just remember this poem, which states the spelling rule.

I before *e*,
Except after *c*,
Or when sounded as *a*,
As in *neighbor* and *weigh*.

Words with *ie*	Words with *cei*	Words with long *a* sound	
chief	receive	neighbor	vein
piece	ceiling	weigh	reign

There are a few exceptions to the rule:

height	neither	seize
foreign	either	leisure

Find the misspelled words in the paragraphs. Cross out each word that is spelled incorrectly. Write the correct spelling above the word.

Example: I believe the ~~hieght~~ is 10 feet.
                        height

To make a long story breif, my friend Aretha recieved a sleigh for her birthday. Not a sled, a sleigh. She shreiked with joy! "I was relieved," she told me, "that my horse, Big Red, nieghed happily when he saw it."

Big Red has achieved stardom in our nieghborhood.

Aretha's favorite liesure activity is riding across the feilds in the sliegh. I don't perceive this as unusual iether!

For You to Do: Choose a story in today's newspaper to read. Look for words with either *ie* or *ei*. Circle the words. Then write them in lists according to the vowel sound *ie* or *ei* spells.

UNIT 4 *WORKING WITH WORDS*   33

Root Words

A root word is a base word or word part. You can often figure out the meaning of an unfamiliar word by first finding a familiar root word within it.

Example: The root word *danger* can be found in **danger**ous and en**danger**ed.

A Circle the root words in the words in the left column. Then match the words to their meanings on the right.

1. report   ____   a. to carry in from another country

2. portable   ____   b. able to be carried

3. transport   ____   c. to carry back and repeat, such as news

4. import   ____   d. to carry or send to another country

5. export   ____   e. to carry from one place to another

What is the root word?   _____

What does the root word mean?   _____

6. dictate   ____   f. to tell beforehand

7. contradict   ____   g. manner of speaking

8. diction   ____   h. to speak against

9. dictionary   ____   i. to tell so that another may write down

10. predict   ____   j. a reference book in which the words of a language are listed with their meanings

What is the root word?   _____

What does the root word mean?   _____

B Figure out the meaning of each of the following words.

1. If *bi* means "two," and *ped* means "foot," what is a biped?

_____

2. If *pseudo* means "false," and *nym* means "name," what is a pseudonym?

_____

3. If *psycho* means "mind," and *ology* means "the study of," what is psychology?

_____

Prefixes

Many words begin with prefixes. A *prefix* is a word part that is added at the beginning of a root word.

> The prefix *pre-* means "before."
> **Pre**heat means "to heat before using."

A Match the words in the left column with their meanings on the right.

1. preview   _____   a. to judge before you have all the evidence
2. prehistoric   _____   b. to go or come before
3. prejudge   _____   c. an essay that comes before the main part of a book
4. predict   _____   d. to tell beforehand
5. prearrange   _____   e. to pay for in advance
6. preface   _____   f. to see before other people
7. precede   _____   g. before historical records were kept
8. prepay   _____   h. to arrange beforehand

> The prefix *re-* means "again" or "back."
> **Re**appear means "to appear again."

B Match the words in the left column with their meanings on the right.

1. repeat   _____   a. to bring back to a former or normal condition
2. repay   _____   b. to arrange again
3. review   _____   c. to look at or study again
4. reunion   _____   d. to go or move backward
5. rearrange   _____   e. a gathering together again
6. recede   _____   f. to pay back
7. restore   _____   g. to get back something lost or taken away
8. recover   _____   h. to do or make again

Negative Prefixes

The prefixes *un-, in,* and *dis-* mean "not" or "the opposite of."

Circle the prefixes in the words in the left column. Then match the words with their meanings on the right.

1. unpack	____	a. safe
2. unnecessary	____	b. closed
3. unopened	____	c. take things out
4. untrue	____	d. not needed
5. unharmed	____	e. false

What is the prefix? _____

What does the prefix mean? _____

_____

6. incorrect	____	f. not dependent on another
7. invisible	____	g. not truthful
8. inactive	____	h. wrong
9. insincere	____	i. not active
10. independent	____	j. not in sight

What is the prefix?_____

What does the prefix mean?_____

_____

11. dishonesty	____	k. not faithful
12. disloyal	____	l. to have an opinion against
13. disorderly	____	m. to feel no confidence in
14. disapprove	____	n. not neat
15. distrust	____	o. lack of truthful behavior

What is the prefix? _____

What does the prefix mean? _____

For You to Do: Make a list of all the words you can think of that have the prefixes *pre-, re-, un-, in-,* and *dis-*. Write a short definition for each word.

Suffixes

A *suffix* is a word part that is added to the end of a root word.

Example: The suffix *-or* means "person or thing that does something."
                An act**or** is a person who acts.

Circle the suffixes in the words in the left column. Then match the
words to their meanings on the right.

1. caller   _____   **a.** one who governs

2. worker   _____   **b.** one who guards

3. governor   _____   **c.** one who calls

4. sailor   _____   **d.** one who works with machines

5. protector   _____   **e.** one who works

6. typist   _____   **f.** one who makes a tour

7. tourist   _____   **g.** one who types

8. machinist   _____   **h.** one who sails

What are the suffixes?_____

What do the suffixes mean?_____

---

9. greatness   _____   **i.** state of well-being

10. kindness   _____   **j.** act of putting into words

11. happiness   _____   **k.** state of enjoying anything

12. arrangement   _____   **l.** act of directing

13. excitement   _____   **m.** condition of being much above average

14. enjoyment   _____   **n.** state of being excited

15. direction   _____   **o.** a kind act

16. expression   _____   **p.** state of being arranged

What are the suffixes?   _____

What do the suffixes mean?   _____

More Suffixes

Some suffixes change words into adjectives.

wash—verb
washable—adjective
  "able to be washed"
	color—noun
	colorful—adjective
	  "full of color"
	colorless—adjective
	  "without color"
		child—noun
		childish—adjective
		  "like a child"

A Write the opposite of each word. Use *-ful* or *-less.*

1. hopeless _____

2. meaningful _____

3. careless _____

4. thoughtful _____

B Circle the suffixes in the words on the left. Then match the words to their meanings on the right.

1. enjoyable _____ a. able to be packed

2. packable _____ b. like a wolf

3. readable _____ c. somewhat brown

4. brownish _____ d. able to be read

5. wolfish _____ e. able to be enjoyed

C Fill in the blanks with the correct words.

1. A new puppy can be _____ to watch. (enjoyable, enjoyment)

2. Teenagers like to _____. (sociology, socialize)

3. The company and the union came to a _____ agreement. (peaceable, peacefulness)

4. The _____ took a bow. (active, actor)

5. Leaves in the fall are _____. (colorful, colorless)

6. Paco learned about cells in _____ class. (biologist, biology)

7. Fresh paint would _____ this room. (beautiful, beautify)

8. To make a cake, follow these _____. (directors, directions)

Review Unit 4

 A Proofread this paragraph. There are capitalization and spelling mistakes. Apostrophes have been left out. Rewrite the paragraph. Correct all the mistakes.

Wont you please come with me to the ice capades? The next show begins at 8 oclock. Ive got two tickets. Some of the skatters are very powerrful. Im just a beginer myself, but I like to skate. I use my friend Emily's skates since she outgrew them. Shes my nieghbor. I know youll like the skating show as much as I do.

_____

_____

_____

_____

_____

_____

_____

_____

_____

B Circle the prefix or suffix in each word. Write the meaning of the word on the line.

1. reread   _____

2. government _____

3. aimless   _____

4. untie   _____

5. owner   _____

6. predate   _____

Homophones

Some of the most commonly mixed-up words in English are *homophones.* Homophones are words that sound the same but have different meanings and different spellings.

Example: **there**   There goes George.
their   Their new car is nice.
they're   They're leaving in a few minutes.

Read the meanings of each pair of words. Then complete each sentence with the correct word.

weather   the general condition of the atmosphere at a certain time and place
whether   a word used to introduce an indirect question or an alternative

1. I don't know _____ to go or not.

2. In May the _____ was windy and warm.

past   a former time
passed   the past tense of the verb *pass;* went by; succeeded in

3. Yolanda was thrilled to find she had _____ her math test.

4. In the _____ Cleo lived in Philadelphia.

5. Every morning on his way to school, David _____ by the field.

brakes   something that stops or slows the motion of something else
breaks   separates into pieces

6. Fine china _____ very easily.

7. Ralph's car skidded when he stepped on the _____.

all ready   completely prepared
already   before; previously

8. Quinton has _____ completed his homework.

9. Are you _____ for the party?

ate   the past tense of the verb *eat*
eight   a number; one more than seven, one less than nine

10. Rita counted out _____ knives, forks, and spoons.

11. Last night we _____ dinner at a Chinese restaurant.

More Homophones

Here are a few more commonly used homophones:

■ Read the meanings of each set of words. Then complete each sentence with the correct word.

weak   lacking in strength; frail
week   a period of time equal to seven days

1. What do you have planned for this _____?

2. Joan felt _____ after she had the flu.

principal   main, most important; the head of a school; amount of money
                    owed as a debt
principle   a rule of conduct; a basic truth or main fact

3. Only part of the car payment is _____; the rest is interest.

4. One _____ Don believes in is the importance of honesty.

5. The _____ river of the United States is the Mississippi.

6. Mrs. Carrido was a popular _____ at Somerset School.

to   in a direction toward; a word used with the infinitive form of a verb
too   very; also
two   a number; one more than one

7. Last night it was _____ cold and wet for our walk.

8. In _____ more days we will leave for Texas.

9. Claudia wanted _____ learn to fly an airplane.

10. In the summer we usually walk _____ the pool.

hear   to perceive sound through the ears
here   at or in this place

11. Bring the book over _____, please.

12. Excuse me, I can't quite _____ you.

through   in one side and out the other; among; from the beginning to the
                   end of; completely to the end
threw   caused to fly through the air

13. Mom! Liz _____ away my papers again!

14. Are you _____ with the dishes yet?

Easily Confused Words

Many words in English are very similar in sound and/or spelling to other words. These words are easier to work with if you pronounce and use them carefully.

■ Read the definitions. Say the words aloud. Complete the sentences with the correct words.

probably   an adverb meaning "most likely"
probable   an adjective meaning "likely to happen or to be true"

1. Since Mike didn't know where he was going, it was _____ that he would get lost.

2. Since Mike doesn't know where he is going, he will _____ get lost.

effect   the result; the influence something has on something else
affect   to produce a change in; to influence

3. The weather does _____ different people in different ways.

4. The _____ of the weather on each person is different.

then   at that time; after that
than   a word used to introduce a comparison

5. Glenn is taller _____ his brother Ted.

6. We bought our tickets and _____ saw the movie.

quiet   silent; calm; motionless
quite   completely; entirely

7. I think the meeting was _____ successful.

8. The night was so _____ you could hear the stars twinkling.

advice   an opinion about how to solve a problem; guidance
advise   to offer advice; to counsel

9. Please give me some _____ about what to do.

10. Please _____ me about what to do.

choose   to pick out; to select (present tense)
chose   picked out; selected (past tense)

11. The captain of the team _____ the players last week.

12. "Which dress do you _____?" asks the salesclerk.

More Easily Confused Words

We make mistakes with similar words when we are in a hurry. "Take your time" is a good rule of thumb.

■ Read the definitions. Say the words aloud. Complete the sentences with the correct words.

later	the comparative form of *late;* after the expected or usual time
latter	the second of two things or events
ladder	a device used for climbing

1. Randy seemed to arrive _____ every day.

2. "Bring the _____ over here," said the roofer.

3. Do you prefer the former or the _____?

formerly	in earlier times; once
formally	according to the rules

4. A business letter is written _____.

5. Our family _____ lived in Philadelphia.

accept	to receive willingly
except	left out; other than

6. Elias decided to _____ the challenge.

7. Everyone _____ Diana arrived on time.

its	the possessive form of *it* (*its* does not have an apostrophe)
it's	contraction of *it is* or *it has* (an apostrophe replaces the letter or letters left out)

8. The puppy whined because _____ bone was missing.

9. Where is _____ bone?

10. _____ behind the sofa.

whose	the possessive form of *who* and *which*
who's	contraction of *who is* or *who has*

11. _____ that girl sitting behind Jaime?

12. I found a glove. Does anyone know _____ it is?

Review Unit 5

A Replace each of the underlined words with another word that means nearly the same. Use a dictionary for help.

Elena <u>looked</u> out her window. She could hardly believe it, but there was a young bald eagle in her front yard. The eagle was <u>wounded</u>. Because she was a veterinarian who specialized in the care of wildlife, Elena knew what to do. She <u>carefully</u> approached the young bird. She talked very <u>softly</u>. She moved very <u>slowly</u>. She wrapped the bird in a soft towel and <u>carried</u> it into the <u>house</u>. "We'll <u>soon</u> have you feeling better," she said.

B Cross out every misspelled word. Write the correct word above it.

Elena called the City Zoo for advise. Soon the young bald eagle found itself in a car rapidly traveling to the zoo, where their was an animal hospital. Elena didn't know weather the young bird would survive or not. They past a field where Elena saw another eagle. "Whose that?" she said out loud. "A friend of yours?" Elena was afraid because the eagle seemed so week. "Just hang in they're! Do you here me?" she said too the bird.

C Continue the story of Elena and the injured eagle. Write what you think happened next.

_____

_____

_____

_____

_____

_____

Working with Sentences

There are a few rules that you need to know about sentences.

> Every sentence expresses a complete thought.

A Write *Yes* on the line if the group of words is a sentence. Write *No* if the group of words is not a sentence. If you wrote *No,* rewrite the words to make them a sentence.

_____ 1. Gone with the wind.

_____

_____ 2. My hairdryer is broken.

_____

_____ 3. Her new sweatshirt is purple.

_____

_____ 4. Lucky number three.

_____

_____ 5. My favorite quotation.

_____

_____ 6. The workers enjoyed using the computer.

_____

> Every sentence begins with a capital letter.

B Capitalize the first word in each sentence. Cross out the lowercase letter. Write the correction above it.

in the eighteenth century, James Watt built a steam engine. that

invention revolutionized travel. in the twentieth century, engineers and

scientists are working on space travel. spacecraft may one day make regular

trips between Earth and the moon or Earth and other planets. do you think

you will ever travel in space? that would certainly be exciting.

The first word of every sentence must be capitalized.

So I should start every sentence with a capital letter, right?

C Rewrite these sentences. Capitalize the first word of each sentence.

1. begin your sentence with a capital letter, please.

_____

2. an Apple is a type of computer.

_____

3. wipe the mud off your shoes, Sam. thanks.

_____

4. did anyone see the pencil with my name on it?

_____

5. the mail carrier usually comes at about one o'clock.

_____

> Every sentence ends with a punctuation mark.
> Never end a sentence with a comma.

D Find the end of each sentence. Add a punctuation mark. Use a period (.), a question mark (?), or an exclamation point (!). Do not use commas to end sentences.

In the morning at five o'clock, the alarm clock rings It is really too early for anyone to wake up Don't you agree I have a clock radio I listen to music for a while Finally, I have to get up Wow What a pain

The first thing I do is make coffee A cup of coffee is the only thing that really wakes me up Do you like coffee I just love that rich, warm taste

Every sentence ends with an end punctuation mark.

Punctuation marks are like road signs. A period, a question mark, or an exclamation point says STOP. A comma says SLOW DOWN or PAUSE. A sentence's end punctuation depends on what type of sentence it is.

➤ Statements end with a period.   My name is Sheila.

➤ Commands or requests end with periods, too.   Please pass the butter.

➤ Questions end with question marks.   What's your name?

➤ Exclamations express strong feelings.   It is a beautiful day!
They end with exclamation points.

E Identify each sentence as a *Statement,* a *Command* or *Request,* a *Question,* or an *Exclamation.* Write your answer on the line before the sentence. Add the correct punctuation mark at the end of each sentence.

_____ **1.** That noise is driving me crazy

_____ **2.** Please stop that noise

_____ **3.** This music is not noise

_____ **4.** It sounds like noise to me

_____ **5.** Why won't you give this music a chance

_____ **6.** Give my music a chance first

_____ **7.** Oh, no, I can't stand opera

_____ **8.** Can we compromise

_____ **9.** I'll listen to your music if you'll listen to mine

_____ **10.** Turnabout is fair play, I always say

_____ **11.** So who gets to go first

_____ **12.** It was my idea, so I do

For You to Do: **1.** Write two examples of each kind of sentence on your own paper.
2. Try to make your sentences tell a story.

Compound Sentences

A compound sentence is made up of two related sentences joined together by a conjunction.

Conjunctions that connect two sentences are *and, but, or, nor,* and *for.* You cannot connect two sentences with only a comma.

Wrong: Bully is a Labrador retriever, Coco is a toy poodle.
Right: Bully is a Labrador retriever, **and** Coco is a toy poodle.
Right: Bully is a Labrador retriever. Coco is a toy poodle.

A Read each group of words. Write *Right* on the line by the number if the words are correctly written as a sentence. Write *Wrong* on the line if they are not. Use the other lines to rewrite the *Wrong* ones correctly.

_____   1.   Jerry and Sue like tennis they play as often as they can.

_____

_____   2.   Write in complete sentences, your writing will improve.

_____

_____   3.   Many afternoons we met at the park, and we played until dark.

_____

_____   4.   Last night Tom read for several hours today he is sleepy.

_____

B Rewrite each pair of sentences to make a compound sentence. Remember to add a conjunction. Underline the conjunction.

1. Renee plays basketball. She hopes her team will win the championship.

_____

_____

2. Bill and Raoul met at the gym. They both lifted weights.

_____

_____

3. I did everything I could. The computer still doesn't work.

_____

_____

Review Unit 6

Always check the sentences that you write.

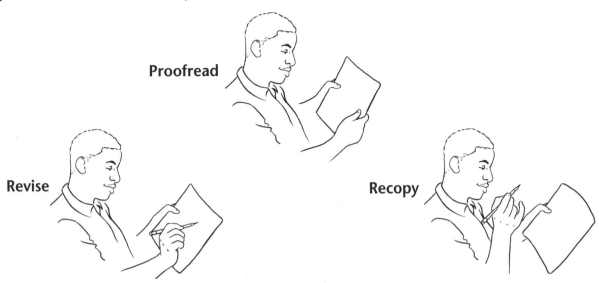

Proofread

Revise

Recopy

Read the story. Find the mistakes. Rewrite the story correctly.

in the spring Alicia decided to play soccer her new team practiced Tuesday and Thursday afternoons they met at Spring Lake Sports Park. Have you ever heard of it. The park was built by the city government for the people to use her coaches decided Alicia would be a good goalie, she was happy because that was her favorite position

_____

_____

_____

_____

_____

_____

_____

_____

_____

_____

_____

Favorite Things

Making lists is one of our most common everyday writing tasks. In this unit, you will practice making some lists.

Example: **My Favorite Books**
1. <u>The Westing Game</u> by Ellen Raskin
2. <u>Treasure Island</u> by Robert Louis Stevenson
3. <u>A Wrinkle in Time</u> by Madeleine L'Engle

Capitalize the first word and all important words in all titles.
Underline the titles of books.

A Make a list of the titles of your five favorite movies.

Underline the titles of movies.

Example: <u>Mission Impossible</u>

1. _____
2. _____
3. _____
4. _____
5. _____

B Make a list of the titles of your five favorite songs. Include the names of the people who sang the songs.

Put quotation marks around the titles of songs.

Example: "Can You Feel the Love Tonight?" by Elton John and Tim Rice

1. _____
2. _____
3. _____
4. _____
5. _____

Shopping for Groceries

Many people shop for groceries once a week. All during the week, they write down things they need to remember to buy when they are at the store.

A Make a grocery list using Monday's menus. Be sure to get everything you need.

Monday's Menus

Breakfast	Lunch	Dinner
eggs	cheese sandwich	tossed salad
bacon	with mustard	green beans
cereal	pickles	rice
milk	carrot sticks	lamb chops
juice	milk	hot tea with lemon
toast	applesauce	vanilla pudding

_____ _____ _____

_____ _____ _____

_____ _____ _____

_____ _____ _____

_____ _____ _____

_____ _____ _____

_____ _____ _____

_____ _____ _____

B Imagine that you are setting up your own apartment. Make a list of all the grocery items you might need.

Examples: soap, sugar, coffee

_____ _____ _____

_____ _____ _____

_____ _____ _____

_____ _____ _____

_____ _____ _____

_____ _____ _____

Shopping at the Drugstore

Most people do some shopping at their local drugstore.

A Make a list of at least 10 items you might buy at a drugstore.

Examples: toothpaste, magazine, film

1. _____   6. _____
2. _____   7. _____
3. _____   8. _____
4. _____   9. _____
5. _____   10. _____

B Here is Maria's shopping list. Check the spelling of each word in a dictionary. Copy the list over correctly.

1. deturgent _____   6. batterys _____
2. tissues _____   7. dog food _____
3. shempoo _____   8. envalopes _____
4. vitimins _____   9. birthdya card _____
5. asprin _____   10. scissors _____

C During the week, Darrell writes down things to do. On Saturday, he runs his errands and does his shopping. Recopy Darrell's list or make one of your own.

Pick up milk and bread   Pick up pizza for dinner
Rent movie at the video store   Return library books
Get oil changed in car   Take dog to vet for shot
Take suit to dry cleaners   Shop for new shoes

Things to Do

_____

_____

_____

_____

_____

A Week's Plan

Here is Juan's list of things to do:

Monday
Do laundry
Get milk at store
Get birthday card for Aunt Marietta
Call Jim
Buy toothpaste
Go to dentist appointment 3 P.M.

■ Try to think ahead. Write down things you need to do each day this week.

Sunday	Monday	Tuesday	Wednesday
_____	_____	_____	_____
_____	_____	_____	_____
_____	_____	_____	_____
_____	_____	_____	_____
_____	_____	_____	_____
_____	_____	_____	_____
_____	_____	_____	_____

Thursday	Friday	Saturday
_____	_____	_____
_____	_____	_____
_____	_____	_____
_____	_____	_____
_____	_____	_____
_____	_____	_____
_____	_____	_____

Packing for Your Vacation

When you go on a vacation, you pack a suitcase with clothes. You probably also put aside some other things to take.

Examples:

books to read

games

address book

A Write all the things you would want to pack in your suitcase.

_____ _____
_____ _____
_____ _____
_____ _____
_____ _____
_____ _____
_____ _____

B Write other things you would like to take with you.

_____ _____
_____ _____
_____ _____
_____ _____
_____ _____
_____ _____
_____ _____

For You to Do: Look through old newspapers and magazines to find examples of lists. Cut them out. Compare them to see the different ways that lists can be made.

Planning a Party

A Write the names of at least 10 people that you would like to invite to your party.

_____   _____

_____   _____

_____   _____

_____   _____

_____   _____

_____   _____

B Write your shopping list for your party. Don't forget napkins!

_____   _____

_____   _____

_____   _____

_____   _____

_____   _____

_____   _____

C Write a list of things you need to do before the party.

_____

_____

_____

_____

_____

_____

_____

Homework and Other Projects

Making lists will help you keep track of schoolwork. Write down
> ➤ homework assignments,
> ➤ long-term projects, and
> ➤ other things to do.

Here is Maureen's list:

Math—Page 45, Problems 1–15

English—read Chapters 1–3 in A Tale of Two Cities.

      Answer questions on worksheet for each chapter.

Study for quiz in English tomorrow.

Write up science experiment.

Science Club tonight! Election of officers.

Work on term paper at library, due next week.

Write your own list of things to do today. Then write your list of things to do this week.

Things to do today

Things to do this week

_____

_____

_____

_____

_____

_____

_____

Review Unit 7

A Make a list of the titles of your five favorite TV shows. Underline the titles.

Example: <u>Star Trek</u>

1. _____
2. _____
3. _____
4. _____
5. _____

B Copy Maxim's list carefully. Spell all the words correctly.

Maxim's list: Your copy:

My Favorite Dishes   _____

Cheese enchiladas   _____

Stir-fried vegetables   _____

Spaghetti with meatballs   _____

Dad's tuna casserole   _____

Chicken pot pie   _____

C Just for fun, make a list of everything you would do or buy if you suddenly became a millionaire.

1. _____
2. _____
3. _____
4. _____
5. _____
6. _____
7. _____
8. _____

Putting Things in Order

Nearly everything we do requires us to put things in order. For example, we sort our laundry into piles.

Jason's

Dad's

Mom's

Tina's

towels

In an office, people put papers in order in file cabinets. Usually folders are put in alphabetical order.

In a library, the books are put in order.

Fiction books are arranged according to the last name of the author.

Nonfiction books are put in groups according to subject.

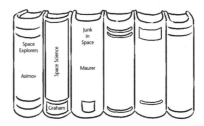

■ There are many ways to put things in order. Name as many ways as you can.

_____

_____

_____

_____

_____

_____

Why is it a good idea to put and keep things in order?

_____

_____

_____

Rules of Order

Here are the two most common ways to put things in order:
> ➤alphabetical order (ABC order)
> ➤chronological order (according to time or date)

A Arrange the words in each list in alphabetical order. Do one list at a time.

Joshua	_____	English	_____
Ryan	_____	French	_____
Aaron	_____	Chinese	_____
Fritz	_____	Russian	_____
Gabriel	_____	Polish	_____

B Arrange the dates and numbers in each list in chronological order. Do one list at a time.

May 8, 1983	_____	1152	_____
August 20, 1980	_____	2012	_____
July 17, 1979	_____	897	_____
January 3, 1983	_____	1401	_____
April 1, 1981	_____	1939	_____

C Arrange these books in order in three ways.

1. alphabetical by title   **2.** by date—earliest to latest   **3.** by length—shortest to longest

Title	Author	Date	Pages
1. *Huckleberry Finn*	Mark Twain	1918	374
2. *Island of the Blue Dolphins*	Scott O'Dell	1960	192
3. *Pride and Prejudice*	Jane Austen	1813	368
4. *Lake Wobegon Days*	Garrison Keillor	1985	337
5. *Little House in the Big Woods*	Laura Ingalls Wilder	1932	256

Alphabetical by Title	**By Date Published (earliest first)**	**By Length (shortest first)**
1. _____	1. _____	1. _____
2. _____	2. _____	2. _____
3. _____	3. _____	3. _____
4. _____	4. _____	4. _____
5. _____	5. _____	5. _____

All Mixed Up

In some lists, words start with different letters. In other lists, words start with the same letter. When two words begin with the same letter, alphabetize by their second letters. If their second letters are the same, alphabetize by their third letters.

Example: Tanya
Teresa
Terry

A Arrange the words in each list in alphabetical order. Work as fast as you can. Do one list at a time.

List 1	List 2	List 3
new _____	lift _____	Lena _____
now _____	letter _____	Lyle _____
none _____	less _____	Lynn _____
nice _____	long _____	Laura _____
nine _____	length _____	Leroy _____

When two words have the same beginning letters, the shorter word comes first. A word without an apostrophe comes before a word with an apostrophe.

Example: are   aren't

B Use all the rules you have learned. Put each of these lists in alphabetical order.

List 1	List 2	List 3
is _____	meat _____	Rosita _____
its _____	me _____	Ramsey _____
it's _____	mean _____	Rufus _____
isn't _____	meant _____	Rachel _____
it _____	meet _____	Rosa _____

Sorting Practice

To become good at sorting, we need practice.

A Sort these foods into three lists according to the meal at which they would most likely be served.

sliced peaches
scrambled eggs and bacon
tossed salad
milk
orange juice

broiled chicken
sweet potatoes
box of raisins
rolls and butter
tuna sandwich

cream of broccoli soup
baked apple
Brussels sprouts
toast and jelly
coffee

Breakfast	**Lunch**	**Dinner**
_____	_____	_____
_____	_____	_____
_____	_____	_____
_____	_____	_____
_____	_____	_____
_____	_____	_____
_____	_____	_____
_____	_____	_____

B Sort the following vegetables. Write the list in order from your most favorite to your least favorite.

corn
peas
beets

tomatoes
green beans
peppers

squash
potatoes
turnips

broccoli
cabbage
radishes

asparagus
lima beans
lettuce

1. _____
2. _____
3. _____
4. _____
5. _____
6. _____
7. _____
8. _____

9. _____
10. _____
11. _____
12. _____
13. _____
14. _____
15. _____

Numerical Order

Sometimes we list things in order according to their numerical value.

A Rewrite the list of clothes according to their cost. List the clothes from the least expensive to the most expensive.

sweater	$25	shoes	$45	cap	$5
T-shirt	$12	socks	$3	jacket	$43
pants	$32	shorts	$15	bathrobe	$24

1. _____   6. _____

2. _____   7. _____

3. _____   8. _____

4. _____   9. _____

5. _____

B This chart lists different kinds of breads and the number of calories in each per serving. Sort the list in two ways.

Breads

dinner roll, 100   Melba toast, 16
cornmeal muffin, 130   rye bread, 66
frozen French toast, 135   white bread, 63
doughnut, 110   pretzel, 7

List the foods according to the number of calories they contain.

—from the most calories to the fewest   —from the fewest calories to the most

1. _____   1. _____

2. _____   2. _____

3. _____   3. _____

4. _____   4. _____

5. _____   5. _____

6. _____   6. _____

7. _____   7. _____

8. _____   8. _____

Review Unit 8

Sorting is important in many different everyday situations. See how quickly and accurately you can sort these lists.

A Sort this list of meats according to the calories they contain. Start with the meat that has the fewest calories per serving.

liver, 200   chicken, 266   turkey, 238
sausage, 80   veal cutlet, 285   frankfurter, 150
steak, 305   ground beef, 328   pork, 319

1. _____   4. _____   7. _____

2. _____   5. _____   8. _____

3. _____   6. _____   9. _____

Isabel's favorite books are

Rebecca of Sunnybrook Farm by Kate Douglas Wiggin
Bridge to Terabithia by Katherine Patterson
Wuthering Heights by Emily Brontë
Gulliver's Travels by Jonathan Swift
Robinson Crusoe by Daniel Defoe
Black Beauty by Anna Sewell
Tom Sawyer by Mark Twain
Little Women by Louisa May Alcott

B Write Isabel's list of books in alphabetical order by title.

1. _____   5. _____

2. _____   6. _____

3. _____   7. _____

4. _____   8. _____

Now list the titles of the books in order by the authors' last names. This is the way you would find the books on a library shelf.

1. _____   5. _____

2. _____   6. _____

3. _____   7. _____

4. _____   8. _____

Getting from Here to There

When you write directions, you should describe each distance and turn carefully.

Examples: Turn right on 4th Street.

or

Go east on Main Street for 2 blocks. Then turn right on 5th Street.

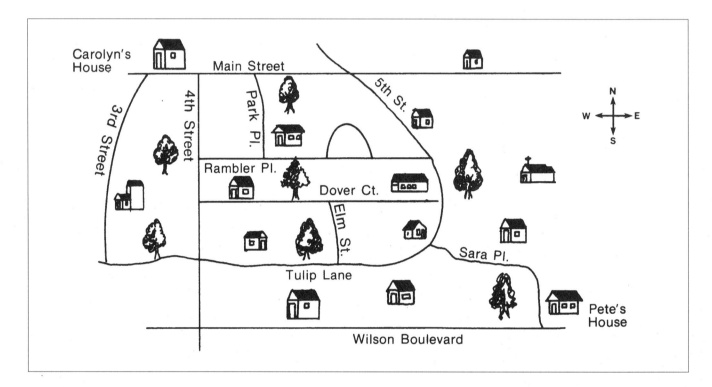

Using the map, write directions about how to get from Carolyn's house to Pete's house.

_____

_____

_____

_____

_____

_____

_____

_____

_____

_____

Writing Directions

In our everyday lives, we often give people directions to our homes.

Here are the directions to Riverview Mall. Study them carefully.

1. Get on the Beltway going south.

2. Go east at Exit 17, George Washington Highway.

3. Drive about 12 miles and then turn north on Cooperstown Road.

4. Go three miles, through two lights, past Cooperstown High School.

5. Turn right at the third light at the gas station.

6. Go two blocks and turn left on Carter Drive.

7. Drive one-and-a-half blocks.

8. Look for the entrance by the large sign on your right.

Write directions to a community place—shopping center, post office, fire department. Start from where you are right now.

_____

_____

_____

_____

_____

_____

_____

_____

_____

_____

_____

_____

_____

_____

Exchange your paper with a friend. Ask whether the directions are clear.

UNIT 9

People often make a map to show others how to get to their homes.

Here is an example:

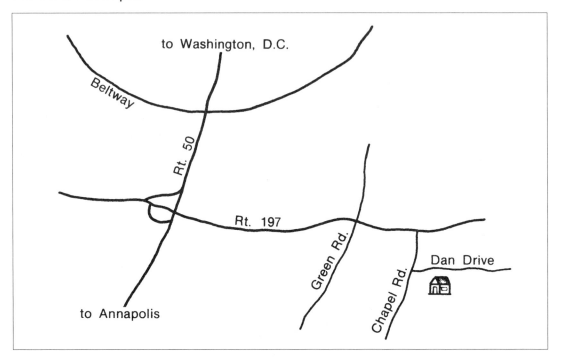

Use the space to draw a map showing how to get from where you are right now to your home.

Recording Directions

Recording directions requires you to be a careful listener.

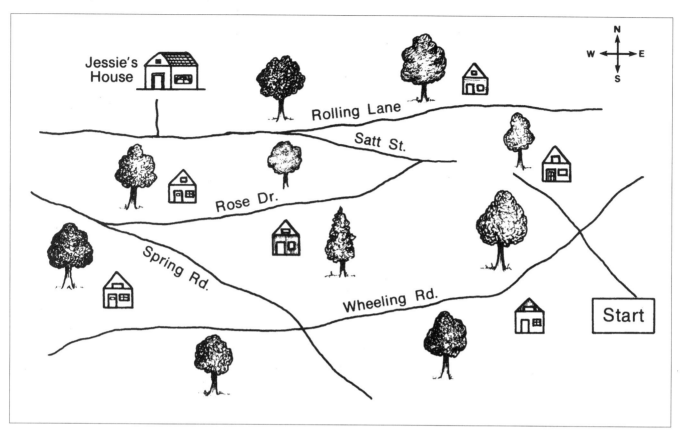

Ask someone to use the map to give you directions to Jessie's house, beginning at *Start.* You are to write the directions as they are given to you. Write the directions on the lines.

_____

_____

_____

_____

_____

_____

_____

Try using your directions with the map. Do they work?

Review Unit 9

Incomplete or confusing directions will get you or your friends lost.

 Study the map. Read the directions about how to go from Emma's house to Anna's house. Edit and revise the directions to make them clearer and easier to follow. Write the revised directions on the lines.

1. Drive southeast on Nelson Street. Cross Roger's Rd.

2. Turn on Rte. 70 and watch for the court.

3. Go right. Then turn on Rose Lane. Look for my house.

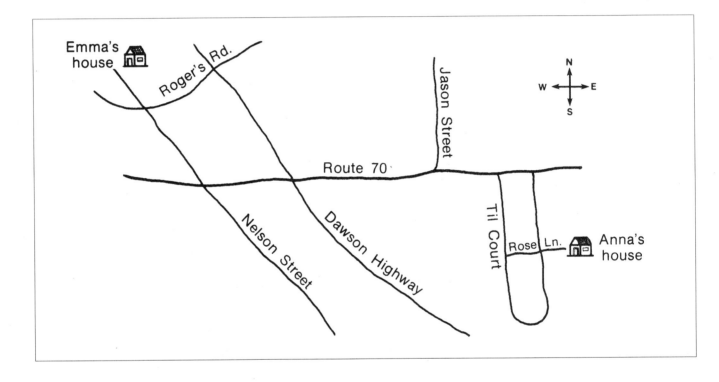

_____

_____

_____

_____

_____

_____

_____

_____

Is It Complete?

In our everyday lives, we often write messages.

A *message* is an informal written communication. We often call it a *note*. A *memo* (short for *memorandum*) is a formal written message used in a business situation.

Kinds of information to include in a message:

➤ Name of the person the message is for

➤ Name of the person the message is from

➤ Time and date the message is written

➤ Facts for the person to know

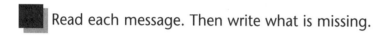 Read each message. Then write what is missing.

Example: Mom. I'll be home later. Ted

_____The time and date of the message are missing._____

1. Ted. Sorry I missed you. Mom

_____

2. Ann. Martin called. Call him back. Sara

_____

3. Mr. Chang. I stopped by to find out about my homework assignment, but you were out. I'll come back later.

_____

4. Dad. Someone called about your meeting. Ted

_____

UNIT 10

A Read the conversation.

Juanita: I am going to be late.

Carmen: Where are you?

Juanita: I'm still at school at band practice. We have to rehearse for at least another hour.

Carmen: When will you be home?

Juanita: Rehearsal should be over at 5 P.M., but I need a ride home. Have Dad pick me up.

Carmen: He's not home yet, and I'm going out.

Juanita: Please leave him a message.

Carmen: OK. See you at dinner.

Write the message here:

Message

B Write a message to a friend. Tell about tonight's homework. Include the time and date. Be sure to include your name and your friend's name. WRITE NEATLY!

Recording Homework Assignments

Sometimes you need to write messages to yourself. Take just as much time and be just as careful as you would if the note were for someone else.

▪ Using the example, fill in the forms with your own information.

SUBJECT: French I

TIME: 10:05

DATE: Monday

ASSIGNMENT: Composition due on Friday. Write one page in French about my favorite food, history of the food, how it got started, how to make it, etc. Ideas??? Pizza—did it come from Italy? When?

SUBJECT: _____

TIME: _____

DATE: _____

ASSIGNMENT: _____

_____

_____

SUBJECT: _____

TIME: _____

DATE: _____

ASSIGNMENT: _____

_____

_____

SUBJECT: _____

TIME: _____

DATE: _____

ASSIGNMENT: _____

_____

_____

UNIT 10

At a job, messages are often taken for other people. Many times the company will have a formal message pad.

■ Use the information to fill in the message forms.

Mr. Ventura
Molly called at 3 P.M., March 3, and wants you to call her back at 555-3423.

To _____
Date _____   Time _____

WHILE YOU WERE OUT

M _____

of _____

Phone _____

Area Code   Number   Extension

TELEPHONED		PLEASE CALL	
CALLED TO SEE YOU		WILL CALL AGAIN	
	RETURNED YOUR CALL		

Message_____

_____

_____

_____

_____

Mr. Lee
Mrs. Miller stopped by to see you. She wants to order a dozen roses. Send them to her house, Friday, March 12.

To _____
Date _____   Time _____

WHILE YOU WERE OUT

M _____

of _____

Phone _____

Area Code   Number   Extension

TELEPHONED		PLEASE CALL	
CALLED TO SEE YOU		WILL CALL AGAIN	
	RETURNED YOUR CALL		

Message_____

_____

_____

_____

_____

Ads and Announcements

The word *ad* is a shortened form of the word *advertisement.* We are familiar with commercials on television and radio. We have all seen ads in magazines and newspapers. Commercials and ads try to sell products or services to people.

An *announcement* is a public message. Announcements are used to tell about upcoming events. An announcement on the school's public address system might tell about a special event that day. A flyer handed out on street corners or a poster displayed in store windows might tell about an upcoming concert.

Here are some guidelines for advertising:

> ➤ Make the message short and to the point.
> ➤ Include all the necessary details.
> ➤ Include some attention-getting words.
> ➤ Be sure it is accurate in every way.

A You want to sell a used book or some other object. Write an advertisement for a newspaper. Keep the ad under 25 words.

_____

_____

_____

_____

_____

_____

B Write an announcement to be made on the public address system. Tell everyone that auditions will be held for a play. Include the date, time, and place. Make everyone want to come.

_____

_____

_____

_____

_____

_____

Writing Ads

What do you want to sell? You may be able to sell it by putting an advertisement in your local newspaper.

A Study the sample ads.

Automobiles, Domestic
JEEP—'49, CJ3 ex-military jeep, 230 V–6 eng. Excel. shape. $1,600. Call 555-1245.
LAMONT—Town car, 4DR, white on white w/red leather interior. Special value $18,000. Visit Rodney's Used Car Center, 1900 South Boulevard.

In the box, write your own ad to sell a car. You may use some of the words or phrases suggested below.

Suggestions: Orig. owner (original owner). New tires. Good condition. MUST SELL! Fully loaded. Only driven on Sundays. Like new. Very clean. Great buy! Well maintained. Best offer. Fully equipped. Specially priced.

B Write an advertisement for a garage sale. Describe things you no longer need or want that you want to sell. Write the ad in the box. Keep it to 50 words or less.

Review Unit 10

 Do this memo and message have all the information they should? Proofread, revise, and recopy the memo and message. Be sure to correct any mistakes and add any missing information.

Mr. Reid called Ms. Davi at 3:00 P.M. on Thursday, May 13. Sherri answered the phone and told him Ms. Davi was out of the office. Mr. Reid asked that Ms. Davi call him back as soon as possible at 1-312-555-4672. Sherri wrote this memo:

To: Ms. Davi	
Date:	Time: 3 p.m.
Mr. Reid called. He wants you to call him back at 1-312-555-6472.	

To: _____

Date: _____ Time: _____

_____

_____

_____

_____

_____

_____

Mrs. Sanchez called home. Juan answered the phone. Mrs. Sanchez asked him to remind Rosa to pick her up at the office at 5:30 P.M. Juan was going out, so he wrote this message:

Mom called. Don't forgit to pick her up at 5:00.
Juan

_____

_____

_____

_____

_____

_____

UNIT 11

We leave a message or a memo, but we usually put letters in the mail.

There are two kinds of letters: personal and business.

Personal Letter

The form is very simple.

Date

May 3

Greeting — Dear Anita,

We are looking forward to your visit with us next week. It's been such a long time since we've seen each other. I hope you plan to stay at least a week.

Please let us know exactly what time to pick you up at the bus stop.

Body

Closing → Love,

Signature → *Florence*

Business Letter

The form has more parts.

Heading

12 Harrison Drive
Sanders, MO 64088
May 3, 1996

Mrs. Carla Tower
Johnson Press
One Silver Circle
Washington, D.C. 20002

Inside Address

Greeting — Dear Mrs. Tower:

I am enclosing a short story for your consideration. It is about a young boy on his first camping trip. Enclosed is a self-addressed, stamped envelope for its return.

Body

Closing → Sincerely yours,

Signature → *Howard D'Mara*

Howard D'Mara

Do you know the parts of a letter? Match the letter parts in the first column with their names in the second column.

1. Sincerely yours,   ____   a. Addressee

2. Dear Anita,   ____   b. Body

3. I am enclosing a...   ____   c. Greeting

4. Mrs. Carla Tower   ____   d. Return address

5. 12 Harrison Drive   ____   e. Closing
   Sanders, OH 64088

A Thank-You Note

People today use the telephone to communicate with their friends more often than they write letters. However, a thank-you note is expected in certain situations. It is polite to write a note to thank people when they give you a gift or when you have been a guest in their home.

Study the sample note.

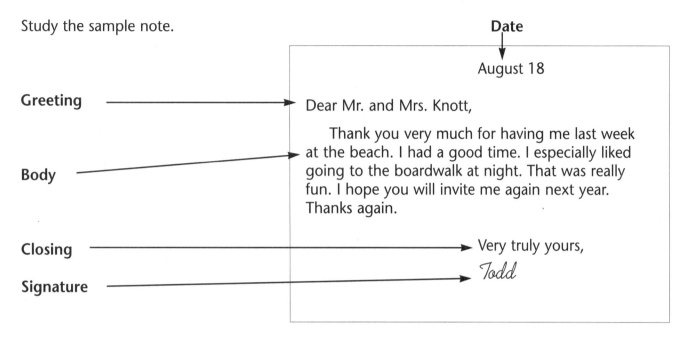

Date

August 18

Greeting

Dear Mr. and Mrs. Knott,

Body

    Thank you very much for having me last week at the beach. I had a good time. I especially liked going to the boardwalk at night. That was really fun. I hope you will invite me again next year. Thanks again.

Closing

Very truly yours,

Signature

Todd

Write a thank-you note to someone you know.

Suggestions: Thank someone who gave you a present on your last birthday.
Thank someone who invited you to a party.
Thank someone who did something nice for you.

UNIT 11

If you want to invite people to an event, you can buy packages of invitations at the store, or you can write your own.

Include this kind of information:
- ➤ the event (party, weekend, dinner)
- ➤ the time and date
- ➤ the place
- ➤ the cost (if any)
- ➤ what the person should bring or wear

Dear Club Members:

    You are invited to an Open House on Monday, March 10, at 7:30 P.M. Come to the Laurel Woods Community Center. Punch and cookies will be served. Dress casually.

                    Sincerely,
                    The Open House Committee

 Read the invitation. Look for mistakes and make corrections. Add missing information. Rewrite the invitation in the box. Use your imagination to add the information that Ramon left out.

Dear Arturo, I'm having a party and I'd like you to come. Bring potato chips and sodas. Let me know if you can come. Ramon

---

Addressing an Envelope

If you do not address the envelope correctly, your letter may never arrive at its destination. Also, be sure to put the right amount of postage on the letter.

Return address
Your name　———▶　Norman Lewis
Your street address　———▶　23 Taber Lane
City, State, ZIP Code　———▶　Rosedale, MD 20840

Addressee　———————————▶　Ms. Tara Gillan
Street address　———————————▶　4320 W. Grover Drive, Apt. 101
City, State, ZIP Code　———————————▶　Camp Hill, PA 17011

These addresses have mistakes in them. Rewrite them correctly.

1. Tang, Aiko

   1231 Santa Anna Parkway

   San Jose, 95129

   CA

   _____
   _____
   _____

2. Ivan Aleshire, Apt. 3A

   Grifton, NC 28530

   Johnson Drive 552

   _____
   _____
   _____

3. Vito Kochert

   6034 Heatherwood Drive, VA

   Alexandria, 22310

   _____
   _____
   _____

4. Stacy Matthews

   21234 Dawson Street

   Alaska, Apt. 2

   Juneau 99801

   _____
   _____
   _____

5. Roy Theuret

   16510

   12 Howard Place

   Erie PA

   _____
   _____
   _____

U N I T 11

General Rules for Business Letters:

➤ Use 8 1/2" by 11" stationery.
➤ Type all copy.
➤ Use only one side of the paper.

The greeting, or salutation, in a business letter includes the title and last name of the addressee.

Dear Dr. Vereb:
Dear Mr. Smith:
Dear Rev. Leonard:

Choose your favorite closing. Here are some examples:

Sincerely,   Sincerely yours,   Very truly yours,
Cordially,   Yours truly,   Respectfully yours,

Label each part of this business letter. Use the words at the bottom of the page.

Vantage Systems
900 West Collington Road
Suite 100
Washington, D.C. 20002

January 12, 1996

Ms. Ann Sawada
4023 Wharton Drive
Collegeville, PA 19426

Dear Ms. Sawada:

Vantage Systems is pleased to offer you the position of office manager starting January 23. Your company benefits are explained in the policy brochure, which I have attached. We are looking forward to having you join us.

Sincerely yours,

Linda Owens

Linda Owens
Personnel Manager

Enclosure

A. _____

B. _____

C. _____

D. _____

E. _____
F. _____
G. _____

typed name and title   inside address   salutation   body
closing   signature   heading

A Letter of Application

One type of business letter is a letter of application. You write this letter when you apply for a job.

 Study the sample help-wanted ad from a newspaper. Write a letter asking for the job. Address an envelope for the letter. Use your own name and address for the heading and the return address.

> OFFICE HELPER WANTED. We are looking for someone willing to work in a small office. Duties include filing, running errands, and helping our busy staff. Write a letter of application to Best Office Supplies, c/o Lacy Marks, 9000 Van Buren Blvd., Suite 12, Reading, MA.

Special Kinds of Letters

Letter to the Editor

One way you can express your opinions is by writing a letter to the editor of a newspaper. The editor will often print your letter if you write it neatly and express your ideas clearly.

Letter of Complaint

People often order items through the mail. If you return an item that you don't like, you will need to explain what is wrong with the product.

Dear Sir or Madam:

In my opinion, the city should definitely build a new ball park. The current one does not have enough seating capacity to attract a major ball team. We have been without a team for many years now.

Yours truly,

Julie Larson

Julie Larson

Dear Sir or Madam:

I am returning the sweater I ordered. It does not look at all like the one pictured in the catalog. I would like you to refund my money.

Sincerely yours,

Oliver Allyn

Oliver Allyn

Write either a letter to the editor or a letter of complaint. Make up the name and address of the addressee.

_____

_____

_____

_____

_____

_____

_____

_____

_____

_____

_____

_____

_____

_____

Review Unit 11

 Proofread, revise, and recopy the business letter. Be sure the greeting and closing are appropriate for a business letter. Check the spelling and sentence structure. Use a dictionary if necessary. Be sure the letter has all its parts!

Mr. Manolo Ramos
Flint, Michigan 48504
2121 Howard Road
April 3, 1996

1213 Superior Lane
George Wilson & Sons, Realty Company
Flint, Michigan 48504

Hi! Mr. Wilson:

As we discussed on the telephone, i'd like you to seel our house. We hope to move from the area within the next two months, the price of the house will include the rugs, all appliances, and the drapes and curtains, and we are having the house painted as you suggested and that should be finished this week.

See you all later,
Manolo

_____

_____

_____

_____

_____

_____

_____

_____

_____

_____

_____

_____

_____

_____

_____

_____

Filling Out an Order Form

In our everyday lives, we fill out many different kinds of forms. Here are three basic rules:

1. Fill in every space. Answer every question. Decide how many to order.
2. Be sure the information is accurate.
3. Write neatly. Print with a pen, or type.

A Fill in the following form for ordering address labels. Order as many labels as you wish.

Complete this form and mail to:		Thomasina Rivera, Inc. Box 5555 Grand Central Station New York, NY 10163	
How Many?	**Name and Address, 3 lines**	**Price**	**Total**
		$2.50 per hundred	

B Answer these questions about the form.

1. Did you write your full name? _____
2. What is your house number? _____
3. What is the name of your street? _____
4. If you live in an apartment, what is the number? _____
5. Did you include the names of your city and state? _____
6. Did you include the ZIP Code? _____
7. What is the name of your city? _____
8. What is the name of your state? _____
9. What is your ZIP Code? _____
10. What is the two-letter abbreviation for your state? _____

The Job Application

One important form that you will fill out is a job application form. The way you fill out this form can help determine whether or not you get a job interview.

1. Fill in every space. Answer every question.
2. Be sure the information is accurate.
3. Write neatly. Print with a pen, or type.

Usually a job application form has four types of questions to answer:

1. Personal Information—questions about you
2. Educational Background—your schooling
3. Work Experience—jobs you have had
4. References—people who know about you, your work, your credit

If a question does not apply to you, write N/A, the abbreviation for *not applicable,* in the space.

 Complete this practice application form. Use information about yourself.

PERSONAL INFORMATION: Please type or print.

Name _Jordan,_____Nancy_____H._____ Phone_(912)__883-5555_____

         Last   First   Middle   (area code)   (number)

Address _17 Vantage Lane_____Albany,_____GA_____31707_____

         Number   Street   City   State   ZIP Code

Social Security Number __571-36-2605_____ Are you a U.S. Citizen? _X_ Yes ____ No

Date of birth __5-10-60_____ Place of birth __Belleville, IL_____

PERSONAL INFORMATION: Please type or print.

Name _____ Phone_____

         Last   First   Middle   (area code)   (number)

Address _____

         Number   Street   City   State   ZIP Code

Social Security Number _____ Are you a U.S. Citizen? ____ Yes ____ No

Date of birth _____ Place of birth _____

Your educational background includes all of the schools you have attended. Your employer may wish to obtain your transcripts. A *transcript* is an official list of the courses you have taken and the grades you received.

 Complete this practice application form. Write about your education.

	Elementary	High	College/ University	Graduate/Professional
School Name and Location	Central School Springdale, PA	Albany H.S. Albany, GA	Melville Junior College Melville, GA	
Years Completed (Circle)	4 5 6 7 ⑧	9 10 11 ⑫	1 ② 3 4	1 2 3 4
Diploma/ Degree **Describe Course of Study:**		June 1996 Academic	A.A. June 1998 Communications	
Describe Specialized Training: Art classes, Albany Art Center, 5 years				
List Other Skills: Drawing, lettering				

	Elementary	High	College/ University	Graduate/Professional
School Name and Location				
Years Completed (Circle)	4 5 6 7 8	9 10 11 12	1 2 3 4	1 2 3 4
Diploma/ Degree **Describe Course of Study:**				
Describe Specialized Training:				
List Other Skills:				

Work Experience

Your work experience includes all the jobs you have ever had. You can also list volunteer work experience for which you were not paid. Keep a record of your employment history in case you ever decide to change jobs.

Employment History
List each job held. Start with your present or last job. Include military service assignments and volunteer activities.

1

Employer:	Daley's Machine Repair	Dates		Work Performed
Address:	161 Grove Street	From	To	repairing stereo components
	Evansville, IN	2/98	present	
Job Title:	radio repair technician	Hrly. Rate/Salary		
		Starting	Final	
Supervisor:	Clifford Daley	$10.75/hr	$12.00/hr	
Reason for Leaving:	N/A			

2

Employer:	Top TV and Radio	Dates		Work Performed
Address:	480 Baughn Avenue	From	To	electronics sales
	Evansville, IN	12/96	2/98	
Job Title:	sales associate	Hrly. Rate/Salary		
		Starting	Final	
Supervisor:	John Heitmann	$7.50/hr	$9.00/hr	
Reason for Leaving:	To accept better position			

■ Complete the practice application form. Write about your work experience.

Employer:	Dates		Work Performed
Address:	From	To	
Job Title:	Hrly. Rate/Salary		
	Starting	Final	
Supervisor:			
Reason for Leaving:			

Employer:	Dates		Work Performed
Address:	From	To	
Job Title:	Hrly. Rate/Salary		
	Starting	Final	
Supervisor:			
Reason for Leaving:			

References

A reference is a recommendation from a person who knows you. Be sure to use only people who will give you a "good" report. Always call these people to ask whether you may use their names as references.

There are three kinds of references:

> ➤ Work references—people who know about your job skills
> ➤ Credit references—people who know about your bill-paying history
> ➤ Personal references—people who know about your character

Work references are former and current employers or teachers.
Credit references are people who have loaned you money, such as a bank or a store.
Personal references can be clergy, neighbors, teachers, and other people who have known you for a long time. Do not ask a relative to be a reference.

A Complete the practice application form. Give information about people who know you.

REFERENCES			
Name	**Address**	**Phone**	**Position**
JoAnna Philipson	1422 Maple Avenue	(502) 349-5740	optometrist
	Bowling Green, KY 42401		
Derrick Lambert	101 South Cosgrove	(502) 282-6746	ophthalmologist
	Bowling Green, KY 42403		

REFERENCES			
Name	**Address**	**Phone**	**Position**

B Fill in each blank with one of the words at the bottom of the page.

1. Felipe asked his _____ for a job _____.

2. When will you be _____ to begin your new _____?

3. What is your current _____?

salary	available	supervisor
position	reference	transcript

Abbreviations on Forms

Lesson 6

Read the instructions on a form very carefully. Be especially careful about abbreviations. Most forms use abbreviations to save space.

Common Abbreviations

No. or #	Number	P.O. Box	Post Office Box
Tel. No.	Telephone Number	POB	Post Office Box
Ext. or X	Telephone Extension Number	Acct.	Account
D.O.B.	Date of Birth	Mo.	Month
M.I.	Middle Initial	Yr.	Year
Soc. Sec. #	Social Security Number	Apt.	Apartment

A Complete the following form. Use the list of abbreviations to help you.

Bank Card Application Form

NAME _____

      Last   First   M.I.

ADDRESS _____

      No.   Street   Apt. #

_____

      City   State   ZIP

SOC. SEC. NO. ____ - ____ - _____   D.O.B. __/__/__

TEL. NO. _____   EXT. _____

OTHER ACCT. WITH THIS BANK?   ( ) Yes   ( ) No

If yes, # _____

Do you wish to apply for a Bank Chg. Acct?   ( ) Yes   ( ) No

B Rewrite each of the following phrases. Write out any abbreviations.

1. Bank Acct. No._____

2. POB 34_____

3. SOC. SEC. #_____

4. Apt. 101_____

5. 249-1330 Ext. 34_____

UNIT 12

UNIT 12 *COMPLETING FORMS* **89**

Writing Checks

Study the sample check. Every blank has been filled in.

```
Charlotte A. Marmo                                        786
4590 Tulip Drive
Elizabethtown, PA 17022
(717) 357-5555                              May 3        19 98

PAY TO THE
ORDER OF    Suburban Furniture                    $ 125.35

   One hundred twenty-five and 35/100——————————— DOLLARS

First National Bank
FOR  lamps                    Charlotte A. Marmo

|| ■ 0 0333 2 || ■   ■ ■ 0 5 2 0 0 0 6 1 8 ■        6 2 6 59 3 6 || ■
```

A Answer these questions about the sample check.

1. What is the check number? _____

2. What is the date on this check? _____

3. Who can cash this check? _____

4. What is the amount of this check? _____

5. What is this check for? _____

6. Who wrote this check? _____

B Fill out the check. Charlotte needs to pay the Electric Company $47.04.
Use today's date.

```
Charlotte A. Marmo                                        787
4590 Tulip Drive
Elizabethtown, PA 17022
(717) 357-5555                            _____ 19 ____

PAY TO THE
ORDER OF   _____   $ _____

   _____ DOLLARS

First National Bank
FOR  _____    _____

|| ■ 0 0333 2 || ■   ■ ■ 0 5 2 0 0 0 6 1 8 ■        6 2 6 59 3 6 || ■
```

Number Words on Checks

On a check you write the amount of money twice. First, you write the amount in numbers. Then you write the amount in words.

Number Words

one	seven	thirteen	nineteen	fifty	one hundred one
two	eight	fourteen	twenty	sixty	two hundred
three	nine	fifteen	twenty-one	seventy	one thousand
four	ten	sixteen	thirty	eighty	one thousand, one
five	eleven	seventeen	thirty-one	ninety	hundred, one
six	twelve	eighteen	forty	one hundred	

A Write out each of the following amounts.

Example:　　$25.30　　Twenty-five dollars and thirty cents

1. $35.99 _____

2. $315.00 _____

3. $9.11 _____

4. $57.90 _____

B Fill out the check. Charlotte needs to pay Peebles Department Store $87.83 for a winter coat. Use today's date.

Charlotte A. Marmo　　　　　　　　　　　788
4590 Tulip Drive
Elizabethtown, PA 17022
(717) 357-5555
　　　　　　　　　　　　　　　　　　_____19____

PAY TO THE
ORDER OF　_____　$ _____

_____ DOLLARS

First National Bank
FOR _____　_____

|| ■ 0 0333 2 || ■　■ ■ 0 5 2 0 0 0 6 1 8 ■　　　6 2 6 59 3 6 || ■

C Write these number words correctly.

1. Fourty-nine dolars no cents　_____

2. Ninty-nine dollars and three sents　_____

3. Twelfe dollars and elven cents　_____

4. Eighten dollars and nine cints　_____

Review Unit 12

Remember the three rules for filling out forms—
1. Fill in every space. Answer every question.
2. Be sure the information is accurate.
3. Write neatly. Print with a pen, or type.

 Fill out the credit card application form. Use information about yourself. When you have finished, be sure to proofread and check your work.

CREDIT CARD APPLICATION

PERSONAL INFORMATION (please print)

First Name	Middle Initial	Last Name

Home Phone ( )	Social Security Number	Date of Birth / /

Street Address	City	State	Zip

Do you ❑Own ❑ Rent	Time at Residence Yrs. Mos.	Monthly Rent $ Mortgage Payments $

Number of Dependents (Excl. Self)

FINANCIAL/EMPLOYMENT INFORMATION (please print)

Current Employer	Business Phone ( )	Position/ Occupation	Length of Employment

Street Address	City	State	Zip

Total Annual Income	Do you ❑ have a checking account ❑ savings account

End-of-Book Test

Proofreading

A Read the paragraph. Look for spelling, capitalization, and punctuation mistakes. Write your corrections in the paragraph.

Dear Cassie

How are you. Its been a long time since I've herd from you. i'm OK.

But now that winter is allmost over, Im alreddy starting to think about

vacation! Do you remimber what fun we had last summer at Aunt sara's

ranch lets meet there agin this year. maybe we'd better start practicing

hour horsebac riding now! Wouldnt it be grate to ride up into the

mountans and camp overnight? I can't wait

love,

Leeann

Adding Endings

B Rewrite each word. Add the ending to the word. Remember, you may need to double the final consonant or drop the final *e.*

1. dance + er   _____
2. love + ly   _____
3. place + ed   _____
4. swim + ing   _____
5. bad + ly   _____
6. begin + er   _____
7. fine + ness   _____
8. admit + ed   _____
9. open + ed   _____
10. paint + er   _____

11. sun + y   _____
12. grace + ful   _____
13. plan + ed   _____
14. teach + ing   _____
15. believe + ed   _____
16. fit + ness   _____
17. run + er   _____
18. write + ing   _____
19. care + less   _____
20. dine + ing   _____

Syllables

C Rewrite each word. Divide it into syllables.

Example: message   mes • age

1. recover   _____   6. honey   _____

2. backpack   _____   7. territory   _____

3. excitement   _____   8. pinch   _____

4. bridge   _____   9. ocean   _____

5. comment   _____   10. revolution _____

Prefixes and Suffixes

D Circle the prefix or suffix in each word. Then match the words with their meanings.

1. preconceived   _____   a. condition of being unhappy

2. painless   _____   b. one who drives a vehicle

3. sadness   _____   c. able to give comfort

4. disrespect   _____   d. formed an opinion beforehand

5. driver   _____   e. condition of being surprised

6. uncertain   _____   f. without pain

7. amazement   _____   g. lack of respect; rudeness

8. comfortable   _____   h. not certain; doubtful

Homophones and Easily Confused Words

E Complete each sentence with the correct word.

| accept | weather | through | effect | weak | all ready |
| except | whether | threw | affect | week | already |

1. The boys took the shortcut _____ the woods.

2. The rain and the cold had no _____ on the runner's performance.

3. By six A.M. I was _____ on the road.

4. Suzanne didn't know _____ she should call first or not.

5. Who _____ Jarod would eat cold pizza for breakfast?

6. We saw the comet every night for a _____.

Making Lists

Mai likes to travel. She has already been to Miami, Florida; Chicago, Illinois; the Grand Canyon; San Francisco, California; Yosemite National Park; and Williamsburg, Virginia. She would like to go to New Orleans, Louisiana; Yellowstone National Park; Los Angeles, California; New York City; the Florida Keys; and Mt. Rushmore in South Dakota.

F First, make a list of the places that Mai has already visited. Then make a list of the places that she would like to visit. Finally, make a list of places that *you* would like to visit.

Mai's List	Mai's List	Your List
1. _____	1. _____	1. _____
2. _____	2. _____	2. _____
3. _____	3. _____	3. _____
4. _____	4. _____	4. _____
5. _____	5. _____	5. _____
6. _____	6. _____	6. _____

Sorting

G First, write the names alphabetically by last name. Then write them alphabetically by first name. Finally, write the names according to the people's ages, beginning with the name of the oldest person.

Alice O'Donnell, 31
Sylvester Sillerman, 62
Roberto Dominguez, 54
Mercedes Martinez, 28

Sylvia Marchand, 53
Rosalyn Francioso, 45
Leah Silverberg, 29
Allen Frampton, 30

By Last Name	By First Name	By Age—oldest first
1. _____	1. _____	1. _____
2. _____	2. _____	2. _____
3. _____	3. _____	3. _____
4. _____	4. _____	4. _____
5. _____	5. _____	5. _____
6. _____	6. _____	6. _____
7. _____	7. _____	7. _____
8. _____	8. _____	8. _____

Letter Writing

H Imagine that your Aunt Celia and Uncle David invited you to stay with them last weekend at their house on Lake Cameron. You had a wonderful time. Now that you are home again, you want to write them a thank-you note. Remember, a thank-you note follows the form of a personal letter. Be sure to include a suitable greeting and a closing. Use today's date and your own name. Write your note on the lines.

Completing Forms

I Mr. Feldman needs to pay his electric bill. Houston Power & Light charged him $132.56. The bill arrived on April 28. Mr. Feldman always pays his bills on the first of the month. Fill out the check as though you were Mr. Feldman.

Clarence G. Feldman	2052
14110 Strack Road	
Houston, TX 77069	
(713) 555-5383	_____ 19 _____

PAY TO THE
ORDER OF _____ $ _____

_____ DOLLARS

First State Bank of Texas

FOR _____   _____

⑂ 072252 ⑂ ⑂ 014600817 ⑂   7894635 ⑂